D0560659

From:

WISDOM AND WIT FROM

Poor Richard's Almanack

Benjamin Franklin

PETER PAUPER PRESS, INC.
WHITE PLAINS, NEW YORK

Designed by Karine Syvertsen

Copyright © 2006
Peter Pauper Press, Inc,
202 Mamaroneck Avenue
White Plains, NY 10601
All rights reserved
ISBN 1-59359-939-0
Printed in China
7 6 5 4 3 2 1

Visit us at www.peterpauper.com

Introduction

The wise and witty sayings herein have been gleaned from many different editions of Ben Franklin's *Poor Richard's Almanack*, which he published yearly from 1732 to 1757. Many of the aphorisms and proverbs were original to Franklin; others were borrowed or adapted from other collections, but he usually added his own supremely witty, sometimes cynical, touch.

With the old Almanack
and the old Year,
Leave thy old Vices,
tho' ever so dear.

Ill Customs & bad Advice
are seldom forgotten.

One good Husband is worth two
good Wives; for the scarcer things
are, the more they're valued.

He that riseth late, must trot
all day, and shall scarce
overtake his business at night.

Fish and Visitors stink
after three days.

How few there are who have
courage enough to own
their Faults, or resolution
enough to mend them!

A country man between
two lawyers, is like a fish
between two cats.

———◆———

Who has deceiv'd thee
so oft as thy self?

———◆———

He that can compose
himself, is wiser than he
that composes books.

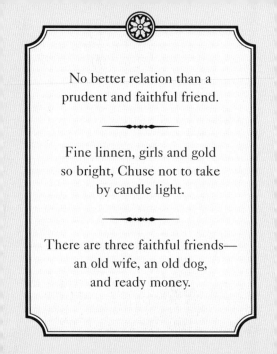

No better relation than a
prudent and faithful friend.

———◆◆◆———

Fine linnen, girls and gold
so bright, Chuse not to take
by candle light.

———◆◆◆———

There are three faithful friends—
an old wife, an old dog,
and ready money.

If Passion drives,
let Reason
hold the Reins.

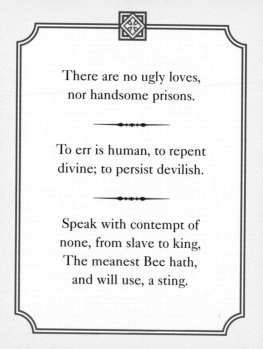

There are no ugly loves,
nor handsome prisons.

To err is human, to repent
divine; to persist devilish.

Speak with contempt of
none, from slave to king,
The meanest Bee hath,
and will use, a sting.

They who have nothing
to trouble them, will be
troubled at nothing.

———◆◆◆———

Beware, beware; he'll cheat without
scruple, who can without fear.

———◆◆◆———

Well done is better than well said.

———◆◆◆———

Keep Conscience clear,
Then never fear.

Doing an Injury puts you
below your Enemy;
Revenging one makes you
but even with him;
Forgiving it sets you above him.

Great Good-nature, without
Prudence, is a great Misfortune.

He that would live in peace and
at ease, must not speak all he
knows, nor judge all he sees.

If you would have guests
merry with cheer, be so yourself,
or so at least appear.

The worst wheel of the cart
makes the most noise.

Necessity never made
a good bargain.

A ship under sail and a
big-bellied woman, are the
handsomest two things
that can be seen common.

The use of money is all the advantage there is in having money.

Ah simple Man! when a boy two precious jewels were given thee, Time and good Advice; one thou hast lost, and the other thrown away.

If you'd be wealthy, think of saving, more than getting: The Indies have not made Spain rich, because her Outgoes equal her Incomes.

He's gone, and forgot
nothing but to say
farewell to his creditors.

Monkeys, warm with envious spite, their most obliging friends will bite.

How many observe Christ's Birth-day; How few his Precepts! O, 'tis easier to keep Holidays than Commandments.

He that drinks his Cyder alone, let him catch his Horse alone.

Wealth is not his that has it,
but his that enjoys it.

'Tis easy to see, hard to foresee.

A little well-gotten will do us
more good, than lordships and
scepters by Rapine and Blood.

In a discreet man's mouth a
publick thing is private.

Old Boys have their Playthings
as well as young Ones;
the Difference is in the Price.

Nor eye in a letter,
nor hand in a purse,
nor ear in the secret of another.

Those who in quarrels interpose,
must often wipe a bloody nose.

Quarrels never could last long,
if on one side only lay the wrong.

What you would seem
to be, be really.

Tart Words make no Friends:
a spoonful of honey will catch more
flies than a Gallon of Vinegar.

Tricks and treachery are the practice of fools that have not wit enough to be honest.

———◆✦◆———

Fear not death; for the sooner we die, the longer shall we be immortal.

———◆✦◆———

There are lazy minds as well as lazy bodies.

There are more old drunkards than old doctors.

Sloth (like Rust) consumes
faster than Labour wears:
the used Key is always bright.

———◆◆◆◆◆———

Hear Reason, or she'll
make you feel her.

———◆◆◆◆◆———

Make haste slowly.

———◆◆◆◆◆———

The Way to see by Faith is to
shut the Eye of Reason.

Drive thy Busin
or it will drive t

———◆◆◆◆◆———

An empty ba
cannot stand up

———◆◆◆◆◆———

What is a Butter
at best he's bu
caterpillar dres
The gaudy Fop's his

Neither a fortress
nor a maidenhead will
hold out long after they
begin to parley.

Observe all men; thyself most.

———◆◆◆———

Wish not so much to live long,
as to live well.

———◆◆◆———

If you have time,
don't wait for time.

———◆◆◆———

There's none deceived
but he that trusts.

None but the well-bred man knows how to confess a fault, or acknowledge himself in an error.

Search others for their virtues, thyself for thy vices.

There is much difference between imitating a good man, and counterfeiting him.

'Tis hard (but glorious)
to be poor and honest.

Clean your Finger,
before you point at my Spots.

He that spills the Rum loses
that only; He that drinks it, often
loses both that and himself.

Wink at small faults—
remember thou hast great ones.

———◆———

Each year one vicious habit
rooted out, in time might make
the worst man good throughout.

———◆———

Pay what you owe, and what
you're worth you'll know.

———◆———

Little Strokes, Fell great Oaks.

Eat to
please thyself,
but dress to
please others.

William, because his wife
was something ill,
Uncertain in her health, indifferent still,
He turn'd her out of doors,
without reply:
I ask'd if he that act could justify.
In sickness and in health,
says he, I am bound
To keep her; when she's worse
or better found,
I'll take her in again;
and now you'll see,
She'll quickly either
mend or end, says he.

Who is strong? He that can
conquer his bad Habits.

A Wolf eats sheep but
now and then;
Ten thousands are
devour'd by men.

Promises may get thee friends,
but non-performance will
turn them into enemies.

Avoid dishonest gain: no price
can recompence the pangs of vice.

Enjoy the present hour, be mindful
of the past; And neither fear nor
wish the approaches of the last.

Different Sects like different clocks,
may be all near the matter,
'tho they don't quite agree.

Proclaim not all thou
knowest, all thou
owest, all thou hast,
nor all thou can'st.

There are three Things
extreamly hard: Steel, a
Diamond, and to know one's self.

———◆·✦·◆———

Be not niggardly of what costs
thee nothing, as courtesy,
counsel, and countenance.

———◆·✦·◆———

Be civil to all; sociable to many;
familiar with few;
Friend to one; Enemy to none.

Sin is not hurtful because it is forbidden, but it is forbidden because it is hurtful.

———◆———

Nor is a duty beneficial because it is commanded, but it is commanded because it is beneficial.

O Lazy bones! Dost thou
think God would have given
thee arms and legs, if he
had not design'd thou
should'st use them?

To bear other people's afflictions,
every one has courage
and enough to spare.

He's a Fool that cannot
conceal his Wisdom.

He who multiplies
Riches multiplies Cares.

An old Man in a House
is a good Sign.

A soft Tongue may strike hard.

You may talk too much
on the best of subjects.

A true Friend is
the best Possession.

No gains without pains.

The same man cannot
be both Friend and Flatterer.

Those who are fear'd, are hated.

Sloth and silence
are a fool's virtues.

———◆◆◆◆◆———

A Brother may not be a Friend,
but a Friend will always
be a Brother.

———◆◆◆◆◆———

Great spenders are bad lenders.

———◆◆◆◆◆———

Many complain of their Memory,
few of their Judgment.

It is wise not
seek a Secret
Honest not t
reveal it.

He who multiplies
Riches multiplies Cares.

An old Man in a House
is a good Sign.

A soft Tongue may strike hard.

You may talk too much
on the best of subjects.

It is wise not to
seek a Secret and
Honest not to
reveal it.

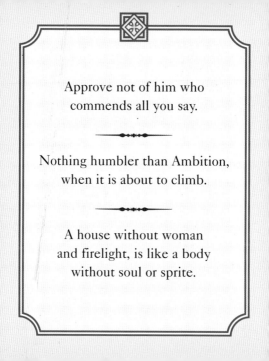

Approve not of him who
commends all you say.

Nothing humbler than Ambition,
when it is about to climb.

A house without woman
and firelight, is like a body
without soul or sprite.

Beware of the young doctor
and the old barber.

He that lieth down with dogs,
shall rise up with fleas.

God works wonders now and then;
Behold! a lawyer, an honest man.

Men and melons are hard to know.

If your head is wax,
don't walk in the Sun.

We are not so sensible of
the greatest Health as of
the least Sickness.

———◆✦◆———

He is ill clothed
that is bare of virtue.

———◆✦◆———

The heart of the fool
is in his mouth,
but the mouth of the wise man
is in his heart.

A Father's a treasure;
a Brother's a comfort;
a Friend is both.

What is Serving God?
'Tis doing Good to Man.

A Slip of the Foot you may soon
recover, but a slip of the Tongue
you may never get over.

Three may keep a secret,
if two of them are dead.

———◆◆◆———

Love your Neighbour;
yet don't pull down your Hedge.

———◆◆◆———

Tongue double, brings Trouble.

———◆◆◆———

He that won't be counsell'd,
can't be help'd.

People who are wrapped up in themselves make small packages.

Lost time is never found again.

Blame-all and Praise-all
are two blockheads.

Beauty and folly are
old companions.

What one relishes, nourishes.

By diligence and patience,
the Mouse bit in two the Cable.

A great Talker may be no Fool,
but he is one that relies on him.

Paintings and Fightings are
best seen at a distance.

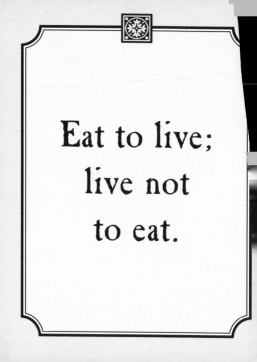

Eat to live;
live not
to eat.

At 20 years of age the will reigns; at 30 the wit; at 40 the judgment.

If you would keep your secret from an enemy, tell it not to a friend.

He is not well bred, that cannot bear Ill-Breeding in others.

Great talkers, little doers.

Wars bring scars.

Beware of little Expenses:
a small Leak will sink a great Ship.

Hear no ill of a friend,
nor speak any of an enemy.

An egg to-day is better
than a hen to-morrow.

Many complain of their Memory,
few of their Judgment.

Great spenders are bad lenders.

A Brother may not be a Friend,
but a Friend will always
be a Brother.

Sloth and silence
are a fool's virtues.

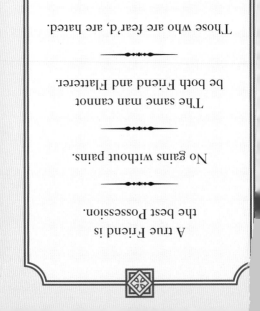

A true Friend is
the best Possession.

No gains without pains.

The same man cannot
be both Friend and Flatterer.

Those who are fear'd, are hated.

An old young man
will be a young old man.

———◆◆◆———

Diligence is the
mother of good luck.

———◆◆◆———

Thou can'st not joke an
enemy into a friend, but thou
may'st a friend into an enemy.

He that
drinks fast,
pays slow.

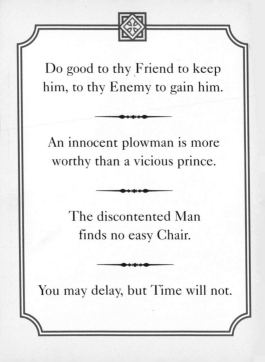

Do good to thy Friend to keep him, to thy Enemy to gain him.

An innocent plowman is more worthy than a vicious prince.

The discontented Man finds no easy Chair.

You may delay, but Time will not.

If you would not be forgotten,
as soon as you are dead and rotten,
either write things worth reading,
or do things worth the writing.

Glass, China, and Reputation,
are easily crack'd, and
never well mended.

God helps them that
help themselves.

A man in a passion
rides a mad horse.

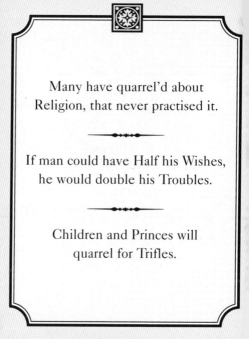

Many have quarrel'd about
Religion, that never practised it.

If man could have Half his Wishes,
he would double his Troubles.

Children and Princes will
quarrel for Trifles.

A false Friend and a
Shadow attend only
while the Sun shines.

Pardoning the Bad,
is injuring the Good.

The doors of Wisdom
are never shut.

Having been poor is no shame,
but being ashamed of it, is.

Blessed is he that expects
nothing, for he shall never
be disappointed.

One To-day is worth
two To-morrows.

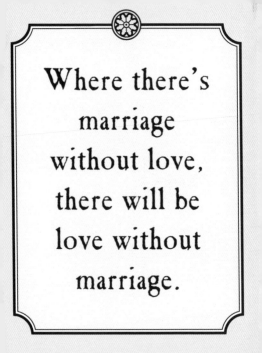

Where there's
marriage
without love,
there will be
love without
marriage.

The Wise and Brave dares
own that he was wrong.

The Proud hate Pride—in others.

If you'd have a servant that
you like, serve yourself.

The rotten apple spoils
his companion.

'Tis easier to prevent bad
habits than to break them.

Silence is not always a
Sign of Wisdom, but
Babbling is ever a Folly.

A long Life may not be
good enough, but a good
Life is long enough.

Bad Gains are true Losses.

———◆◆◆◆———

To be intimate with a foolish
Friend, is like going to
Bed to a Razor.

———◆◆◆◆———

You may sometimes be
much in the wrong, in owning
your being in the right.

Praise little, dispraise less.

Virtue may not always make a
Face handsome, but
Vice will certain make it ugly.

He that's content hath enough.
He that complains hath too much.

A full Belly makes a dull Brain.

Success has ruin'd many a Man.

Haste makes Waste.

To be humble to superiors
is duty, to equals courtesy,
to inferiors nobleness.

Here comes the orator,
with his flood of words,
and his drop of reason.